KIDNEY DIALYSIS

DIET COOKBOOK AND FOOD LIST FOR BEGINNERS

A nutritional guide for rejuvenating renal health with over 100 low-sodium, Potassium Recipes for Patients managing Kidney Disease

Dr. VICTORIA H. MILLER

Copyright © 2024 – Victoria H. Miller
ISBN:
Printed in the United States of America

Disclaimer

All rights reserved. No part of this publication may be reproduced, distributed, or transmitted in any form or by any means, including photocopying, recording, or other electronic or mechanical methods, without the prior written permission of the publisher, except in the case of brief quotations embodied in critical reviews and certain other non-commercial uses permitted by copyright law. For permission requests, write to the publisher, addressed at the address below

TABLE OF CONTENTS

Introduction to Kidney Dialysis 12

Understanding Kidney Function 12

Introduction to Kidney Dialysis.................. 14

The Importance of Diet in Managing Kidney Health 16

The Basics of a Kidney Dialysis Diet 20

Nutritional Needs and Restrictions 20

Reading and Understanding Food Labels 24

Tips for Kidney-Friendly Shopping.............. 29

Food list for kidney dialysis diet 31

Foods to Avoid... 31

Foods to eat... 35

Planning Your Meals 41

Setting Up Your Kitchen for Success 41

Meal Planning Strategies 46

Shopping List Essentials............................... 51

Breakfast Recipes for a Healthy Start 56

Low-Potassium Berry Smoothie 56

Egg White Omelet with Vegetables 57

Apple Cinnamon Rice Cereal 57

Low-Sodium Turkey Bacon and Tomato Sandwich 58

Cranberry Almond Rice Pudding 59

Toasted Bagel with Cream Cheese Alternative 60

Low-Potassium Fruit Salad 61

Vegetable Hash with Egg Whites 62

Vanilla Almond Milk Porridge 63

Cottage Cheese with Berries 64

Peachy Keen Smoothie 64

Savory Muffin Tin Egg Whites 65

Low-Sodium Cheese and Tomato Toast ... 66

Honey-Lime Quinoa Fruit Salad 67

Zucchini and Bell Pepper Frittata 68

Light Bites & Snacks..70

Apple Cinnamon Muffins 70

Zucchini Chips.. 71

Rice Cake with Avocado Spread............. 72

Cucumber Sandwiches 73

Berry Yogurt Parfait 74

Carrot and Hummus Dip 75

Tuna Salad Stuffed Tomatoes 75

Egg Salad on Cucumber Rounds 76

Peach Smoothie 77

Baked Kale Chips 78

Lemon Herb Chicken 79

Quinoa Salad with Veggies........................ 80

Baked Apple Chips 81

Creamy Garlic Mushrooms........................ 82

Pineapple Cucumber Salad 83

Satisfying Soups and Salads..........................84

Low-Sodium Vegetable Soup.....................84

Cucumber and Tomato Salad 86

Chicken Noodle Soup (Low-Sodium)........87

Mixed Greens Salad with Vinaigrette 89

Carrot Ginger Soup..90

Beet and Goat Cheese Salad 92

Creamy Cauliflower Soup 93

Quinoa and Black Bean Salad 95

Spinach and Strawberry Salad 96

Pumpkin Soup...97

Pear and Walnut Salad 99

Asparagus Lemon Soup 101

Mediterranean Chickpea Salad 102

Broccoli and Cauliflower Soup 104

Avocado and Shrimp Salad 106

Main Courses... 108

Beef and Broccoli Stir-Fry 108

Quinoa Vegetable Salad 109

Grilled Salmon with Dill 110

Turkey Vegetable Soup 111

Pasta Primavera....................................... 113

Baked Tilapia with Lemon Pepper 114

Cauliflower Rice Stir-Fry 115

Grilled Veggie Platter................................ 116

Chicken and Rice Casserole 117

Tuna Salad with Greek Yogurt................. 118

Baked Cod with Tomatoes and Olives... 119

Vegetable Quiche (Crustless) 120

Lentil Soup 122

Shrimp and Zucchini Noodles................... 123

Sides and Sauces 125

Cauliflower Mash 125

Carrot and Zucchini Ribbons................... 126

Green Bean Almondine 127

Lemon-Dill Sauce 129

Apple Cucumber Salad 130

Garlic Olive Oil Pasta 131

Honey Mustard Dressing 133

Roasted Bell Peppers 134

Balsamic Vinaigrette 135

Mashed Sweet Potatoes 136

Cilantro Lime Rice 137

Tangy Coleslaw 139

Basil Pesto (Low Sodium) 140

Quinoa Salad with Lemon Vinaigrette ... 142

Steamed Asparagus with Lemon Butter . 144

Desserts and Treats 146

Low-Potassium Apple Crisp 146

Vanilla Rice Pudding 147

Lemon Bars 148

Kidney-Friendly Chocolate Cake 149

Berry Fruit Salad.. 151

Peach Sorbet 151

Almond Biscotti 152

Carrot Cake Muffins 154

Coconut Macaroons 155

Angel Food Cake 156

Pumpkin Spice Muffins 157

Pear and Ginger Crumble 159

Strawberry Gelatin Parfait......................... 160

Chocolate Peanut Butter Balls 161

Blueberry Lemon Muffins............................ 162

Beverages and Smoothies........................**164**

Cranberry Apple Spritzer........................... 164

Blueberry Lemonade Smoothie 165

Cucumber Mint Water 166

Peach Iced Tea (Low Sugar).................... 167

Pineapple Coconut Water 168

Carrot Ginger Juice 169

Strawberry Basil Water 170

Almond Milk Smoothie 171

Herbal Tea Infusion 172

Green Smoothie 173

Lemon Ginger Zinger 174

Berry Blast Smoothie 175

Minty Melon Drink 176

Iced Hibiscus Tea 177

Vanilla Almond Shake 178

Conclusion **180**

Chapter 1

Introduction to Kidney Dialysis

Understanding Kidney Function

Kidney function is at the heart of our body's natural filtration system, playing a pivotal role in maintaining our overall health and well-being. Imagine your body as a sophisticated city, bustling with activity, and your kidneys as the diligent waste management crew, tirelessly working 24/7 to ensure the city remains clean and functional. These bean-shaped organs, tucked away beneath your ribcage, perform the critical task of filtering blood, removing toxins, and balancing fluids, ensuring that your internal environment remains stable against external changes.

The importance of kidneys goes beyond just waste elimination. They are the unsung heroes in the regulation of blood pressure, the guardians of fluid balance, and the custodians of vital nutrients like electrolytes. Moreover, they play a crucial role in producing hormones that guide the production of red blood cells, bolster bone health, and regulate blood pressure. In essence, kidneys are the central hub in the complex network of bodily functions, ensuring that everything runs smoothly and efficiently.

However, like any sophisticated system, the kidneys are vulnerable to damage, especially from chronic conditions such as diabetes and high blood pressure, which can impair their ability to perform these essential functions. When the kidneys are unable to filter blood effectively, harmful levels of fluid and waste can accumulate in the body, leading to kidney disease. This is where the significance of a kidney-friendly diet comes into play, particularly for individuals facing the challenges of kidney disease or undergoing dialysis. A tailored diet not only supports kidney health but also enhances the efficacy of treatment processes, ensuring that the body remains in optimal condition despite the hurdles.

Introduction to Kidney Dialysis

Kidney dialysis stands as a beacon of modern medicine, a testament to the ingenuity of healthcare, and a lifeline for those grappling with kidney disease. This advanced treatment, akin to a guardian angel, steps in when one's kidneys can no longer fulfill their critical role of purifying the blood and regulating body fluids. It's a journey that intertwines science with the human will to persevere, offering hope and a renewed lease on life for many.

Embarking on dialysis is much more than starting a medical procedure; it is a profound transformation in one's healthcare journey, necessitating courage, adaptation, and an unwavering spirit of resilience. The kidneys, our body's natural filtration system, tirelessly work to remove waste and excess fluid, keeping our internal environment in delicate balance. However, when these silent workhorses falter due to disease or injury, dialysis emerges as a crucial bridge, performing the vital functions that the kidneys no longer can.

This intricate process of dialysis does not merely mimic the kidneys' functions; it embodies the pinnacle of medical intervention, enabling individuals to lead fuller, more active lives despite the challenges of kidney failure. It's a narrative of survival, of technology meeting tenacity, where patients find a new rhythm in life, adapting to the rhythms of dialysis sessions, embracing changes in diet and lifestyle, and often, rediscovering themselves in the process.

The Importance of Diet in Managing Kidney Health

Diet plays a pivotal role in managing kidney health, acting as both a preventive measure and a critical component of treatment for those with kidney disease. The kidneys, our body's natural filtration system, are responsible for removing waste products and excess fluid from the blood. They also balance electrolytes, regulate blood pressure, and support the production of red blood cells. When kidney function is compromised, either through chronic kidney disease, acute injury, or other kidney-related health issues, the impact of diet on the body becomes even more pronounced.

A kidney-friendly diet helps to minimize the workload on the kidneys, reducing the accumulation of waste products and fluids in the body. This dietary approach focuses on limiting certain nutrients that can exacerbate kidney damage or strain, including sodium, potassium, phosphorus, and protein. For individuals with kidney disease, especially those on dialysis, adhering to a diet tailored to their specific needs can significantly improve outcomes, enhance quality of life, and even slow the progression of kidney damage.

Sodium is a key focus, as high sodium intake can increase blood pressure, contributing to kidney damage and exacerbating heart disease. Limiting foods high in sodium, such as processed foods, canned goods, and certain restaurant meals, is crucial. Potassium and phosphorus control is also vital; while essential for the body, excessive levels can be harmful when kidney function is impaired. High potassium levels can affect heart rhythm, while too much phosphorus can weaken bones over time.

Protein intake must be carefully managed as well. While essential for growth and repair, excessive protein can increase the burden on the kidneys. The right balance depends on the individual's stage of kidney disease, with dialysis patients often requiring more protein than those not on dialysis.

Moreover, fluid intake is another consideration. In the advanced stages of kidney disease, when the kidneys can no longer effectively remove excess fluid, limiting fluid intake helps prevent swelling, high blood pressure, and heart failure.

Adopting a kidney-friendly diet requires careful planning and education. It involves reading labels, understanding nutrient content, and sometimes, making significant changes to eating habits. However, the benefits are substantial. A well-managed diet can help control symptoms, reduce the risk of complications, enhance the effectiveness of treatment, and ultimately, improve the overall quality of life for those with kidney disease.

Chapter 2

The Basics of a Kidney Dialysis Diet

Nutritional Needs and Restrictions

Navigating the nutritional landscape for individuals with kidney disease involves a delicate balance between meeting the body's needs and avoiding excesses that can exacerbate kidney damage. The nutritional needs and restrictions of those with kidney disease or undergoing dialysis vary significantly from the general population, requiring a tailored approach that considers the unique challenges of managing kidney health.

1. **Nutritional Needs**

Protein: Protein is essential for growth, repair, and the maintenance of good health. However, for individuals with kidney disease, protein intake must be carefully managed. The kidneys help to filter out the waste products of protein metabolism, and when kidney function is compromised, these waste products can build up in the blood. In the early stages of kidney disease, reducing protein intake may help to decrease the workload on the kidneys. Conversely, patients undergoing dialysis may need to increase their protein intake to replace what is lost during the dialysis process.

Energy: Adequate caloric intake is important to maintain energy levels and overall health. People with kidney disease, especially those on dialysis, may have higher energy requirements. A dietitian can help determine the appropriate caloric intake based on individual needs, including activity level and treatment regimen.

Fluids: Fluid balance is crucial in kidney disease management. In the later stages of kidney disease or for those on dialysis, the kidneys may not be able to remove excess fluid, leading to swelling, high blood pressure, and other complications. Fluid intake may need to be restricted to help manage these symptoms.

2. **Nutritional Restrictions**

Sodium: High sodium intake can increase blood pressure and swelling, putting additional strain on the kidneys. Limiting sodium is crucial, which means avoiding high-sodium foods, using less salt in cooking, and reading food labels to make lower-sodium choices.

Potassium: While potassium is vital for nerve and muscle function, too much potassium can be dangerous when kidney function is impaired, as it can lead to heart problems.

Foods high in potassium, such as bananas, oranges, potatoes, and tomatoes, may need to be limited or balanced with other foods.

Phosphorus: Excess phosphorus can lead to bone and heart problems in people with kidney disease, as damaged kidneys can't remove phosphorus efficiently. Phosphorus is found in foods like dairy products, nuts, seeds, and whole grains, and intake may need to be restricted.

Calcium: Calcium needs may vary in kidney disease. Some people may need to limit calcium intake due to phosphorus binders, while others may need to increase it to prevent bone disease. The balance of calcium and phosphorus is crucial for bone health.

Navigating these nutritional needs and restrictions often requires the guidance of a healthcare professional, such as a dietitian specializing in kidney health. A dietitian can help create a personalized eating plan that addresses individual health needs, dietary preferences, and the specific requirements of kidney disease or dialysis treatment. By adhering to this tailored nutritional plan, individuals with kidney disease can better manage their condition, mitigate symptoms, and improve their overall quality of life

Reading and Understanding Food Labels

Reading and understanding food labels is a critical skill for managing kidney health, as it enables individuals to make informed choices about the foods they consume, particularly when navigating the complexities of a kidney-friendly diet.

Here's a guide on how to read and understand food labels, focusing on key nutrients that impact kidney health:

1. Serving Size

- **Start here.** The serving size reflects the amount typically consumed in one sitting and is crucial for accurately assessing the nutritional content of the food. All the nutritional information on the label is based on this serving size.
- **Compare to your portion.** If you eat double the serving size listed, you'll need to double the nutritional values to get an accurate picture of what you're consuming.

2. Calories

- **Energy intake.** This indicates the amount of energy you get from one serving of the food. Balancing calorie intake is essential for maintaining a healthy weight, especially important for individuals with kidney disease.

3. Sodium

- **Limit sodium intake.** High sodium consumption can increase blood pressure and exacerbate kidney and heart conditions. Look for foods with less than 140 mg of sodium per serving, which are considered low sodium.

4. Potassium

- **Monitor potassium levels.** Not all labels list potassium, but it's crucial for those with kidney disease to manage potassium intake. Foods low in potassium have less than 200 mg per serving. More companies are including potassium on labels, so pay attention to this if you need to manage your intake.

5. **Phosphorus**
    - **Phosphorus is often not listed on labels,** but foods high in protein and certain additives (such as phosphates) are generally high in phosphorus. Look for ingredients with "phos" in the name as an indicator of phosphorus content.

6. **Protein**
    - **Protein needs vary.** Those with kidney disease need to manage protein consumption carefully, especially if on dialysis. The amount of protein needed can vary widely based on individual health status and treatment stage.

7. Total Carbohydrates

- **Includes sugars and fibers.** For those with diabetes, managing carbohydrate intake is crucial for controlling blood sugar levels. Fiber is beneficial for heart health, while added sugars should be limited.

8. Total Fat

- **Types of fat matter.** Look for foods low in saturated and trans fats to help manage cholesterol levels and reduce the risk of heart disease. Healthy fats, such as those from fish, nuts, and olive oil, can be beneficial in moderation.

Reading Ingredients Lists

- **Ingredients are listed by quantity,** from highest to lowest. This can help you identify the main components of the food and spot ingredients that may need to be limited, such as added sugars, sodium, and phosphorus-containing additives.

Tips for Kidney-Friendly Shopping

- **Choose fresh or frozen fruits and vegetables** over canned varieties, which may contain added sodium or potassium.
- **Select whole grains** that are lower in phosphorus than their refined counterparts, unless otherwise advised by your healthcare provider.
- **Opt for lean sources of protein** and monitor portion sizes to manage protein intake.
- **Be wary of "reduced" or "low" labels** without checking the actual nutritional content, as they may still be higher than recommended for

certain nutrients like sodium or potassium.

Chapter 3

Food list for kidney dialysis diet

Foods to Avoid

High Potassium Foods

Potassium is a mineral that your body needs to work properly, but too much potassium can be harmful when your kidneys are not fully functional. High levels of potassium can affect your heart rhythm.

- Avocados
- Bananas
- Oranges, orange juice
- Potatoes, sweet potatoes
- Tomatoes, tomato sauce, and tomato-based products
- Spinach, Swiss chard, and other leafy greens

- Dried fruits (apricots, prunes, raisins)
- Melons (cantaloupe, honeydew)
- Pumpkins
- Chocolate

High Phosphorus Foods

Phosphorus is another mineral that needs to be balanced in your diet. Too much phosphorus can lead to bone and cardiovascular problems in kidney dialysis patients.

- Dairy products (milk, cheese, yogurt)
- Nuts and peanut butter
- Seeds
- Beans and lentils
- Whole grains and bran
- Cocoa and beer

- Colas and other beverages with phosphate additives

High Sodium Foods

Sodium is commonly found in many foods and is a major contributor to high blood pressure, which can worsen kidney disease and increase the risk of heart complications.

- Table salt and sea salt
- Canned soups and vegetables
- Processed meats (bacon, ham, sausage, hot dogs)
- Fast food and takeout
- Frozen dinners and pizza
- Snack foods (chips, pretzels, crackers)

- Condiments (soy sauce, ketchup, barbecue sauce)

High Fluid Foods

Fluid intake may need to be restricted for those on dialysis to prevent fluid overload, which can lead to swelling, high blood pressure, and heart issues.

- Soups and broths
- Ice cream and gelato
- Popsicles and frozen treats
- Fruits with high water content (watermelon, strawberries)
- Beverages (water, tea, coffee, soda, alcoholic drinks)

Other Considerations

- **Protein:** While protein is an essential nutrient, dialysis patients need to consume high-quality protein in controlled amounts. Avoid high-fat meats and opt for leaner choices.

- **Added Sugars:** Foods high in added sugars can contribute to calorie intake without providing nutritional value, potentially leading to weight gain and other health issues.

- **Processed and Fast Foods:** Often high in sodium, phosphorus, and unhealthy fats, these foods can exacerbate health problems in dialysis patients.

Foods to eat

Low Potassium Fruits and Vegetables

Potassium levels need to be carefully managed on dialysis. Here are some lower potassium options:

- Apples and apple juice

- Cranberries and cranberry juice
- Grapes and grape juice
- Pineapple and pineapple juice
- Strawberries, blueberries, raspberries
- Plums
- Cabbage
- Cauliflower
- Cucumbers
- Peas
- Green beans
- Bell peppers

High-Quality Protein

Protein is essential for health, especially on dialysis to help repair tissues and maintain muscle mass:

- Egg whites: High in protein and low in phosphorus.
- High-quality meats: Poultry (without the skin), fish, and lean cuts of beef and pork. Fish such as salmon,

mackerel, and tuna are also good sources of heart-healthy omega-3 fatty acids.
- Dialysis patients may need more protein than the average person, but it's important to consume high-quality sources to minimize waste products in the blood.

Low Phosphorus Foods

Managing phosphorus is key to preventing bone disease and maintaining heart health:
- Rice milk, almond milk, or soy milk (unenriched varieties)
- Light-colored soft drinks and lemonade
- Corn and rice cereals
- Pasta, rice, and refined white bread (in moderation and as recommended by a healthcare provider)

Low or Moderate Sodium Foods

Keeping sodium intake low can help manage blood pressure and reduce thirst:

- Fresh or frozen vegetables (without added sauces or seasonings)
- Fresh meats and fish (avoid those injected with sodium solutions)
- Homemade meals where you can control the amount of salt added
- Herbs and spices to flavor food instead of salt

Healthy Fats

Fats are important for overall health, but choosing the right types is key:

- Olive oil, avocado oil, and flaxseed oil
- Avocados (in very small amounts due to their potassium content)
- Small portions of nuts and seeds (be mindful of phosphorus levels)

Carbohydrates

Carbohydrates are a key source of energy, but it's important to choose complex carbs for sustained energy and fiber:

- White bread and pasta (easier for some kidney patients to manage compared to whole grains)
- Rice, especially white rice has less potassium and phosphorus than brown rice
- Cereals made from refined grains, avoiding those with added nuts or chocolate

Fluids

Fluid intake needs to be carefully managed on dialysis to prevent fluid overload:

It's crucial to monitor the amount of fluid consumed, including soups, gelatin, ice cream, and beverages. The fluid allowance may vary based on urine output and dialysis efficiency.

Chapter 4

Planning Your Meals

Setting Up Your Kitchen for Success

Setting up your kitchen for success, especially when managing a specialized diet such as one for kidney dialysis, is key to maintaining your health and simplifying meal preparation. A well-organized kitchen stocked with the right tools and ingredients can make it easier to adhere to your dietary restrictions while still enjoying delicious and nutritious meals.

Here are some tips to optimize your kitchen for health and convenience:

1. Stock Up on Kidney-Friendly Foods

- **Pantry Staples:** Keep low-sodium broth, rice (white or basmati for lower phosphorus content), pasta, and low-sodium canned vegetables. Include olive oil or avocado oil for healthy fats.

- **Spices and Herbs:** Stock a variety of salt-free spice blends, fresh or dried herbs, and lemon juice to enhance flavor without adding sodium or potassium.
- **Refrigerator Essentials:** Fresh or frozen low-potassium vegetables and fruits, egg whites, and lean cuts of meat. Consider dairy alternatives like unenriched almond or rice milk.
- **Freezer Favorites:** Freeze portions of lean proteins, homemade low-sodium soups, and stews for quick meals.

2. Organize the Kitchen for Efficiency

- **Designate Areas:** Have specific areas for kidney-friendly foods to avoid confusion. Keep snacks and ready-to-eat foods within easy reach.

- **Food Prep Station:** Set up a clean, spacious area for washing and preparing vegetables and fruits. Having a dedicated cutting board for fresh produce helps avoid cross-contamination.

- **Cooking Zone:** Organize cooking utensils, pots, pans, and spices near the stove for easy access. Non-stick cookware can reduce the need for cooking oils.

3. Invest in Quality Kitchen Tools

- **Digital Scale:** For precise measurement of ingredients, helping to manage portion sizes and nutritional content.

- **Measuring Cups and Spoons:** Essential for following recipes

accurately, especially when managing nutrient intake.
- **Blender or Food Processor:** Useful for making smoothies, soups, and purees with kidney-friendly ingredients.
- **Slow Cooker or Pressure Cooker:** For easy, one-pot meals that can help retain nutrients without adding unwanted ingredients.

4. Practice Safe Food Storage
- **Labeling:** Clearly label leftovers with dates to ensure they are consumed within a safe timeframe. Use transparent containers to easily identify foods.
- **Freeze in Portions:** Freeze meals in individual portions for easy thawing and to avoid waste.

5. Educational Resources

- Keep a collection of kidney-friendly cookbooks or recipes in your kitchen for inspiration.
- Have a list of websites or apps that offer renal diet recipes and tips for easy reference.

6. Mindful Shopping Habits

- **Plan Ahead:** Make a list of needed items based on your meal planning to avoid impulsive buys that may not fit your dietary needs.
- **Read Labels:** Become proficient in reading and understanding food labels to choose the best options for your kidney health.

7. Routine Kitchen Clean-up

- Keeping your kitchen clean and organized can make meal prep more enjoyable and help you stay on track with your dietary goals. Regularly clean your fridge and pantry to remove expired items or those that no longer fit your diet.

Meal Planning Strategies

Meal planning is a crucial strategy for anyone, especially for individuals with specific dietary needs, such as those on kidney dialysis. Effective meal planning can help manage nutritional intake, reduce stress around meal times, and ensure a varied and enjoyable diet within the constraints of dietary restrictions. Here are comprehensive strategies to help with meal planning:

1. Understand Your Dietary Needs

- **Consult with a Dietitian:** Work closely with a healthcare professional or renal dietitian to understand your specific nutritional requirements and restrictions based on your stage of kidney disease, treatment, and any other health conditions.

2. Start with a Template

- **Create a Weekly Plan:** Develop a basic template for the week that includes all meals and snacks. This structure helps in organizing your shopping list and ensures variety over the week.

3. Build a Recipe Repository

- **Collect Kidney-Friendly Recipes:** Gather recipes that fit your dietary needs. Use cookbooks, online resources, and recommendations from your dietitian.
- **Organize Recipes:** Keep your recipes organized in a binder, digital folder, or app for easy access. Categorize

them by meal type (breakfast, lunch, dinner, snacks) and by the main ingredient for simplicity.

4. Incorporate Variety

- **Rotate Foods:** To avoid dietary boredom and ensure a range of nutrients, rotate through different fruits, vegetables, grains, and protein sources that fit your dietary guidelines.
- **Theme Nights:** Consider theme nights, like "Meatless Monday" or "Fish Friday," to add fun and predictability to your meal planning.

5. Plan for Leftovers

- **Cook in Batches:** Prepare larger portions of meals that can be safely stored and easily reheated. This can save time and energy, especially on

days when cooking feels like a burden.
- **Repurpose Meals:** Plan to use leftovers creatively. For example, a roast chicken can become a chicken salad or a chicken soup base for another meal.

6. Prep in Advance

- **Batch Cooking:** Dedicate time for batch cooking and prepping ingredients. Cooking grains, chopping vegetables, or portioning out protein in advance can streamline meal assembly during the week.
- **Snack Preparation:** Have kidney-friendly snacks prepped and easily accessible to prevent reaching for less suitable options.

7. Flexible Meal Planning

- **Adjust as Needed:** Be prepared to adjust your meal plan based on how you feel, unexpected events, or leftover ingredients that need to be used up to minimize waste.

8. Shopping Smart

- **Organized Shopping List:** Create a shopping list based on your meal plan, organized by store sections (produce, meat, dairy alternatives) to make shopping more efficient.
- **Read Labels:** Always read nutritional labels to ensure the products meet your dietary needs, focusing on sodium, potassium, phosphorus, and protein content.

9. Involve Your Household

- **Engage Family Members:** If you're not living alone, involve household members in meal planning and preparation to make it a shared responsibility and to ensure meals meet everyone's preferences.

10. Review and Reflect

- **Weekly Reviews:** At the end of each week, review what worked well and what didn't. This reflection can help refine future meal plans, reduce food waste, and improve satisfaction with your meals.

Shopping List Essentials

Here's a shopping list, divided into categories, based on typical dietary guidelines for individuals undergoing dialysis.

Fresh Produce

- **Low Potassium Vegetables:** Cauliflower, bell peppers, cabbage, cucumber, eggplant, onions, and garlic.
- **Low Potassium Fruits:** Apples, berries (strawberries, blueberries, raspberries), grapes, and pineapple.

Protein Sources

- **High-Quality Proteins:** Chicken breast (skinless), turkey, lean cuts of beef, pork loin, and fish (e.g., salmon, cod, tilapia). Consider the specific dietary advice regarding omega-3 fatty fish intake.
- **Plant-Based Proteins:** Egg whites (for those who need high-quality protein with less phosphorus).

- **Dairy Alternatives:** Unenriched rice milk or almond milk (check for added phosphorus or calcium).

Grains and Cereals
- **Low Phosphorus Options:** White bread, white rice, pasta, and cereals made from refined grains (avoid whole grains if phosphorus needs to be limited).

Snacks
- **Sodium Snacks:** Unsalted popcorn, rice cakes, and low-sodium crackers.
- **Fruits and Vegetables:** Carrot sticks, cucumber slices, and apple slices are good for snacking.

Cooking Ingredients and Condiments
- **Healthy Oils:** Olive oil and avocado oil for cooking and dressing.
- **Herbs and Spices:** Fresh or dried herbs (basil, oregano, parsley) and spices

(turmeric, paprika) to flavor food without salt.
- **Low Sodium Condiments:** Vinegar, lemon juice, and homemade or low-sodium dressings and sauces.

Beverages
- **Low Potassium Beverages:** Water, clear apple juice, and cranberry juice. Avoid or limit high-potassium fruit juices and sodas, especially colas.
- **Tea and Coffee:** In moderation, depending on fluid restrictions and individual tolerance.

Dairy and Eggs
- **Egg Whites:** For those who require additional high-quality protein without the added phosphorus of whole eggs.

- **Dairy Alternatives:** As mentioned, suitable non-dairy milk alternatives with attention to added minerals.

Frozen and Canned Goods

- **Frozen Vegetables:** Choose those without added sauces or seasonings, focusing on low-potassium options.
- **Canned Goods:** Low sodium or no-salt-added versions of vegetables, fruits in their juice, and tuna or salmon packed in water.

Miscellaneous

- **Dialysis-Friendly Snacks:** Specific products designed for kidney care, available in some health food sections, may offer convenient, safe options.

Chapter 5

Breakfast Recipes for a Healthy Start

Low-Potassium Berry Smoothie

Ingredients:

- 1 cup blueberries (fresh or frozen)
- 1/2 cup strawberries (fresh or frozen)
- 1 cup rice milk or almond milk (unenriched)
- 1 tablespoon honey (optional)

Instructions:

1. Blend all ingredients until smooth.
2. Serve immediately.

Nutritional Information: Approx. 150 calories, 2g protein, 35g carbohydrates, 0g fat, 60mg sodium, 170mg potassium, 100mg phosphorus.

Egg White Omelet with Vegetables

Ingredients:

- 4 egg whites
- 1/2 cup diced bell peppers
- 1/4 cup chopped onions
- 1 teaspoon olive oil
- Salt-free seasoning to taste

Instructions:

1. Sauté vegetables in olive oil until soft.
2. Whisk egg whites and pour over vegetables in the pan. Cook until set.
3. Fold the omelet in half and serve.

Nutritional Information: Approx. 120 calories, 15g protein, 5g carbohydrates, 5g fat, 110mg sodium, 200mg potassium, 60mg phosphorus.

Apple Cinnamon Rice Cereal

Ingredients:

- 1 cup cooked white rice

- 1/2 apple, peeled and diced
- 1/4 teaspoon cinnamon
- 1 cup rice milk or almond milk (unenriched)
- 1 teaspoon honey (optional)

Instructions:

1. Combine all ingredients in a pot and simmer until the apples are soft.
2. Serve warm.

Nutritional Information: Approx. 200 calories, 4g protein, 44g carbohydrates, 1g fat, 55mg sodium, 150mg potassium, 50mg phosphorus.

Low-Sodium Turkey Bacon and Tomato Sandwich

Ingredients:

- 2 slices white bread, toasted
- 2 slices low-sodium turkey bacon, cooked
- 2 slices tomato

- Lettuce leaves

Instructions:
1. Layer turkey bacon, tomato, and lettuce between toasted bread slices.
2. Serve immediately.

Nutritional Information: Approx. 220 calories, 15g protein, 28g carbohydrates, 6g fat, 200mg sodium, 180mg potassium, 90mg phosphorus.

Cranberry Almond Rice Pudding

Ingredients:
- 1 cup cooked white rice
- 1/2 cup cranberries (fresh or dried without added sugar)
- 2 cups almond milk (unenriched)
- 1/4 cup slivered almonds
- 1 tablespoon honey

Instructions:
1. In a pot, combine rice, cranberries, and almond milk. Cook over medium heat until thickened.
2. Stir in almonds and honey before serving.

Nutritional Information: Approx. 250 calories, 5g protein, 50g carbohydrates, 5g fat, 80mg sodium, 150mg potassium, 100mg phosphorus.

Toasted Bagel with Cream Cheese Alternative

Ingredients:
- 1 low-sodium bagel (white or refined grain)
- 2 tablespoons cream cheese alternative (low in phosphorus and potassium)

Instructions:
1. Toast the bagel to your liking.

2. Spread the cream cheese alternative evenly over the bagel halves.

Nutritional Information: Approx. 300 calories, 10g protein, 55g carbohydrates, 2g fat, 180mg sodium, 100mg potassium, 90mg phosphorus.

Low-Potassium Fruit Salad

Ingredients:
- 1/2 cup pineapple chunks
- 1/2 cup grapes
- 1/2 cup peeled apple chunks
- 1 tablespoon lemon juice
- 1 teaspoon honey (optional)

Instructions:
1. Combine all fruits in a bowl.
2. Drizzle with lemon juice and honey. Toss gently to combine.

Nutritional Information: Approx. 100 calories, 1g protein, 25g carbohydrates, 0g fat, 5mg sodium, 180mg potassium, 20mg phosphorus.

Vegetable Hash with Egg Whites

Ingredients:

- 1/2 cup diced potatoes (boiled and drained well)
- 1/4 cup diced bell peppers
- 1/4 cup diced onions
- 4 egg whites
- 1 teaspoon olive oil
- Salt-free seasoning to taste

Instructions:

1. Sauté potatoes, bell peppers, and onions in olive oil until crispy.
2. In another pan, cook egg whites until set and serve on top of the vegetable hash.

Nutritional Information: Approx. 200 calories, 18g protein, 23g carbohydrates, 4g fat,

150mg sodium, 300mg potassium, 100mg phosphorus.

Vanilla Almond Milk Porridge

Ingredients:

- 1 cup almond milk (unenriched)
- 1/2 cup quick-cooking oats
- 1/4 teaspoon vanilla extract
- 1 tablespoon slivered almonds
- 1 teaspoon honey (optional)

Instructions:

1. Bring almond milk to a boil, add oats, and reduce heat to simmer, stirring frequently until cooked.
2. Stir in vanilla extract, and top with almonds and honey.

Nutritional Information: Approx. 200 calories, 6g protein, 34g carbohydrates, 5g fat, 100mg sodium, 200mg potassium, 150mg phosphorus.

Cottage Cheese with Berries

Ingredients:
- 1/2 cup low-sodium cottage cheese
- 1/2 cup mixed berries (strawberries, blueberries, raspberries)

Instructions:
1. Serve cottage cheese topped with mixed berries.

Nutritional Information: Approx. 120 calories, 15g protein, 15g carbohydrates, 0.5g fat, 200mg sodium, 200mg potassium, 150mg phosphorus.

Peachy Keen Smoothie

Ingredients:
- 1 cup frozen peaches
- 1 cup almond milk (unenriched)
- 1 teaspoon honey (optional)
- A pinch of cinnamon

Instructions:
1. Blend all ingredients until smooth.
2. Serve chilled.

Nutritional Information (approximate): 150 calories, 2g protein, 30g carbohydrates, 2g fat, 90mg sodium, 190mg potassium, 50mg phosphorus.

Savory Muffin Tin Egg Whites

Ingredients:
- 8 egg whites
- 1/2 cup diced red bell peppers
- 1/4 cup chopped spinach (excess water removed)
- Salt-free garlic powder to taste

Instructions:
1. Preheat oven to 350°F (175°C). Grease a muffin tin lightly with olive oil.

2. Whisk egg whites with garlic powder. Stir in bell peppers and spinach.
3. Pour mixture into muffin tins, filling each cup about 3/4 full.
4. Bake for 20-25 minutes or until eggs are set.
5. Cool slightly before serving.

Nutritional Information (approximate): 70 calories per muffin, 9g protein, 2g carbohydrates, 0g fat, 110mg sodium, 150mg potassium, 60mg phosphorus.

Low-Sodium Cheese and Tomato Toast

Ingredients:
- 2 slices white or sourdough bread
- 2 slices low-sodium cheese (choose types lower in phosphorus)
- 1 tomato, sliced
- Fresh basil leaves (optional)

Instructions:
1. Toast the bread slices to your preference.
2. Place cheese slices and tomato on one slice of toast. If using a toaster oven, broil briefly to melt the cheese.
3. Top with fresh basil, cover with the second slice of toast and serve warm.

Nutritional Information (approximate):

220 calories, 12g protein, 28g carbohydrates, 8g fat, 200mg sodium, 180mg potassium, 150mg phosphorus.

Honey-Lime Quinoa Fruit Salad

Ingredients:
- 1 cup cooked quinoa (cooled)
- 1/2 cup diced apples
- 1/2 cup diced pears
- 1 tablespoon lime juice
- 1 teaspoon honey

- Mint leaves for garnish

Instructions:
1. In a large bowl, combine the quinoa, apples, and pears.
2. In a small bowl, whisk together lime juice and honey until well blended.
3. Pour the lime-honey dressing over the quinoa fruit mixture and toss gently to combine.
4. Garnish with mint leaves before serving.

Nutritional Information (approximate): 200 calories, 6g protein, 45g carbohydrates, 1g fat, 10mg sodium, 200mg potassium, 100mg phosphorus.

Zucchini and Bell Pepper Frittata

Ingredients:
- 4 egg whites
- 1 small zucchini, thinly sliced

- 1/2 red bell pepper, diced
- 1 tablespoon olive oil
- Salt-free Italian seasoning to taste

Instructions:

1. Preheat oven to 375°F (190°C).
2. In a skillet, heat olive oil over medium heat. Add zucchini and bell pepper; sauté until soft.
3. Whisk egg whites with Italian seasoning and pour over the vegetables in the skillet, stirring gently to combine.
4. Transfer the skillet to the oven and bake until the egg whites are set about 15-20 minutes.
5. Slice and serve warm.

Nutritional Information (approximate): 120 calories, 12g protein, 5g carbohydrates, 7g fat, 100mg sodium, 220mg potassium, 70mg phosphorus.

Chapter 6

Light Bites & Snacks

Apple Cinnamon Muffins

Ingredients:

- 1 ½ cups all-purpose flour
- ½ cup sugar
- 2 tsp baking powder (low sodium)
- ½ tsp cinnamon
- ¼ cup unsalted butter, melted
- ¾ cup unsweetened applesauce
- 2 egg whites

Instructions:

1. Preheat oven to 350°F (175°C).
2. Mix flour, sugar, baking powder, and cinnamon in a bowl.
3. In another bowl, combine melted butter, applesauce, and egg whites.
4. Combine wet and dry ingredients until just mixed.

5. Pour into muffin tins and bake for 20-25 minutes.

Nutritional Information:
- Calories: 150
- Sodium: 50 mg
- Potassium: 60 mg
- Phosphorus: 40 mg

Zucchini Chips

Ingredients:
- 2 large zucchinis
- Olive oil spray
- Garlic powder
- Black pepper

Instructions:
1. Preheat oven to 225°F (105°C).
2. Slice zucchini thinly and lay on a baking sheet.

3. Spray lightly with olive oil and sprinkle with garlic powder and black pepper.
4. Bake for 1-2 hours until crispy.

Nutritional Information:
- Calories: 50
- Sodium: 20 mg
- Potassium: 230 mg
- Phosphorus: 30 mg

Rice Cake with Avocado Spread

Ingredients:
- 1 unsalted rice cake
- ¼ avocado
- Lemon juice
- Black pepper

Instructions:
1. Mash the avocado and mix with a few drops of lemon juice and black pepper.

2. Spread over the rice cake.

Nutritional Information:
- Calories: 120
- Sodium: 15 mg
- Potassium: 250 mg
- Phosphorus: 50 mg

Cucumber Sandwiches

Ingredients:
- Cucumber slices
- Cream cheese (low sodium)
- Dill

Instructions:
1. Spread a thin layer of cream cheese on a cucumber slice.
2. Top with another slice and sprinkle with dill.

Nutritional Information:
- Calories: 35
- Sodium: 40 mg

- Potassium: 70 mg
- Phosphorus: 20 mg

Berry Yogurt Parfait

Ingredients:

- ½ cup Greek yogurt (non-fat, low sodium)
- ¼ cup fresh berries (strawberries, blueberries)
- 1 tbsp honey

Instructions:

1. Layer yogurt, berries, and honey in a glass.

Nutritional Information:

- Calories: 120
- Sodium: 45 mg
- Potassium: 150 mg
- Phosphorus: 100 mg

Carrot and Hummus Dip

Ingredients:
- ¼ cup hummus (low sodium)
- Carrot sticks

Instructions:
1. Serve carrot sticks with hummus for dipping.

Nutritional Information:
- Calories: 70
- Sodium: 130 mg
- Potassium: 220 mg
- Phosphorus: 60 mg

Tuna Salad Stuffed Tomatoes

Ingredients:
- 1 can tuna (in water, low sodium)
- 2 tbsp mayonnaise (low sodium)
- 2 medium tomatoes
- Black pepper
- Fresh parsley

Instructions:
1. Mix tuna with mayonnaise and black pepper.
2. Cut tomatoes in half and scoop out the insides.
3. Fill tomatoes with tuna mixture and garnish with parsley.

Nutritional Information:
- Calories: 150
- Sodium: 190 mg
- Potassium: 300 mg
- Phosphorus: 50 mg

Egg Salad on Cucumber Rounds

Ingredients:
- 2 hard-boiled eggs, chopped
- 1 tbsp mayonnaise (low sodium)
- Cucumber slices
- Paprika

Instructions:
1. Mix chopped eggs with mayonnaise.
2. Place a spoonful of cucumber slices and sprinkle with paprika.

Nutritional Information:
- Calories: 70
- Sodium: 90 mg
- Potassium: 80 mg
- Phosphorus: 60 mg

Peach Smoothie

Ingredients:
- ½ cup frozen peaches
- ½ cup almond milk (unsweetened)
- ½ tsp vanilla extract

Instructions:
1. Blend all ingredients until smooth.

Nutritional Information:
- Calories: 80
- Sodium: 30 mg

- Potassium: 190 mg
- Phosphorus: 25 mg

Baked Kale Chips

Ingredients:
- 1 bunch kale, torn into pieces
- Olive oil spray
- Salt substitute

Instructions:
1. Preheat oven to 300°F (150°C).
2. Lay kale pieces on a baking sheet and lightly spray with olive oil.
3. Sprinkle with salt substitute.
4. Bake for 10-15 minutes until crispy.

Nutritional Information:
- Calories: 60
- Sodium: 50 mg
- Potassium: 150 mg
- Phosphorus: 40 mg

Lemon Herb Chicken

Ingredients:

- 2 boneless, skinless chicken breasts
- 1 tbsp olive oil
- 1 tsp dried oregano
- 1 tsp dried thyme
- Juice of 1 lemon
- Black pepper

Instructions:

1. Preheat the oven to 375°F (190°C).
2. Rub chicken breasts with olive oil, lemon juice, oregano, thyme, and black pepper.
3. Bake in the oven for 25-30 minutes, until cooked through.

Nutritional Information:

- Calories: 165
- Sodium: 70 mg
- Potassium: 220 mg
- Phosphorus: 190 mg

Quinoa Salad with Veggies

Ingredients:

- ½ cup quinoa (rinsed)
- 1 cup water
- ½ cup diced cucumbers
- ½ cup diced bell peppers
- 2 tbsp lemon juice
- 1 tbsp olive oil
- Black pepper
- Fresh herbs (parsley, mint)

Instructions:

1. Cook quinoa in water as per package instructions and let cool.
2. Mix cooked quinoa with cucumbers, bell peppers, lemon juice, olive oil, black pepper, and fresh herbs.

Nutritional Information:

- Calories: 120
- Sodium: 15 mg
- Potassium: 175 mg

- Phosphorus: 95 mg

Baked Apple Chips

Ingredients:

- 2 apples
- Cinnamon

Instructions:

1. Preheat oven to 200°F (90°C).
2. Thinly slice apples and remove seeds.
3. Place slices on a baking sheet and sprinkle with cinnamon.
4. Bake for 1-2 hours, flipping halfway through, until crisp.

Nutritional Information:

- Calories: 95
- Sodium: 2 mg
- Potassium: 194 mg
- Phosphorus: 20 mg

Creamy Garlic Mushrooms

Ingredients:

- 1 cup sliced mushrooms
- 1 tbsp unsalted butter
- 1 clove garlic, minced
- ¼ cup heavy cream (low sodium)
- Black pepper
- Fresh parsley

Instructions:

1. In a skillet, melt butter over medium heat and add garlic and mushrooms. Cook until mushrooms are soft.
2. Add heavy cream, reduce heat to low, and simmer until sauce thickens.
3. Season with black pepper and garnish with parsley.

Nutritional Information:

- Calories: 150
- Sodium: 50 mg
- Potassium: 150 mg

- Phosphorus: 60 mg

Pineapple Cucumber Salad

Ingredients:

- 1 cup diced pineapple
- 1 cup diced cucumber
- 1 tbsp lime juice
- 1 tsp honey
- Fresh mint leaves

Instructions:

1. Combine pineapple, cucumber, lime juice, and honey in a bowl.
2. Chill for at least 30 minutes before serving.
3. Garnish with fresh mint leaves.

Nutritional Information:

- Calories: 70
- Sodium: 5 mg
- Potassium: 120 mg
- Phosphorus: 10 mg

Chapter 7

Satisfying Soups and Salads

Low-Sodium Vegetable Soup

Ingredients:

- 1 cup chopped carrots
- 1 cup diced celery
- 1 cup chopped green beans
- 1/2 cup diced onions
- 2 cloves garlic, minced
- 4 cups low-sodium vegetable broth
- 1 tsp dried thyme
- 1 tsp dried basil
- Olive oil

Instructions:

1. In a large pot, heat a drizzle of olive oil over medium heat. Add onions and garlic, sautéing until softened.
2. Add carrots, celery, and green beans. Cook for 5 minutes.
3. Pour in the vegetable broth, thyme, and basil. Bring to a boil, then simmer for 20-25 minutes.

Nutritional Information:

- Calories: 80
- Sodium: 70 mg
- Potassium: 200 mg
- Phosphorus: 50 mg

Cucumber and Tomato Salad

Ingredients:

- 2 cups sliced cucumbers
- 1 cup diced tomatoes
- 1/4 cup red onion, thinly sliced
- 2 tbsp olive oil
- 1 tbsp vinegar
- Black pepper

Instructions:

1. Combine cucumbers, tomatoes, and red onion in a bowl.
2. Drizzle with olive oil and vinegar. Toss to coat.
3. Season with black pepper to taste.

Nutritional Information:

- Calories: 70

- Sodium: 10 mg
- Potassium: 180 mg
- Phosphorus: 30 mg

Chicken Noodle Soup (Low-Sodium)

Ingredients:

- 2 chicken breasts, cooked and shredded
- 4 cups low-sodium chicken broth
- 1 cup diced carrots
- 1 cup diced celery
- 1/2 cup pasta (egg noodles recommended)
- 1 tsp dried parsley
- Olive oil

Instructions:

1. In a large pot, heat a drizzle of olive oil over medium heat. Add carrots and celery, sautéing until softened.
2. Add chicken broth and bring to a boil. Reduce heat to simmer.
3. Add pasta and chicken. Cook according to pasta package instructions.
4. Stir in parsley before serving.

Nutritional Information:

- Calories: 150
- Sodium: 90 mg
- Potassium: 220 mg
- Phosphorus: 100 mg

Mixed Greens Salad with Vinaigrette

Ingredients:

- 4 cups mixed greens (lettuce, spinach, arugula)
- 1/4 cup sliced almonds
- 1/4 cup dried cranberries
- 2 tbsp balsamic vinegar
- 1 tbsp olive oil
- Black pepper

Instructions:

1. Combine mixed greens, almonds, and dried cranberries in a large bowl.
2. In a small bowl, whisk together balsamic vinegar and olive oil.
3. Drizzle dressing over salad and toss. Season with black pepper.

Nutritional Information:

- Calories: 100
- Sodium: 30 mg
- Potassium: 150 mg
- Phosphorus: 70 mg

Carrot Ginger Soup

Ingredients:

- 2 cups chopped carrots
- 1 tbsp grated ginger
- 1/2 cup chopped onions
- 4 cups low-sodium vegetable broth
- 1 tbsp olive oil
- Black pepper

Instructions:

1. In a pot, heat olive oil over medium heat. Add onions and ginger, cooking until onions are translucent.

2. Add carrots and vegetable broth. Bring to a boil, then simmer until carrots are tender.

3. Puree the soup with an immersion blender. Season with black pepper.

Nutritional Information:

- Calories: 90
- Sodium: 75 mg
- Potassium: 230 mg
- Phosphorus: 40 mg

Beet and Goat Cheese Salad

Ingredients:

- 2 cups mixed greens
- 1/2 cup cooked and sliced beets
- 1/4 cup crumbled goat cheese
- 2 tbsp walnuts, chopped
- 2 tbsp olive oil
- 1 tbsp vinegar
- Black pepper

Instructions:

1. Arrange mixed greens on a plate. Top with sliced beets, goat cheese, and walnuts.
2. In a small bowl, whisk together olive oil and vinegar. Drizzle over the salad.
3. Season with black pepper to taste.

Nutritional Information:

- Calories: 150
- Sodium: 125 mg
- Potassium: 200 mg
- Phosphorus: 80 mg

Creamy Cauliflower Soup

Ingredients:

- 1 head cauliflower, chopped
- 1/2 cup chopped onions
- 2 cloves garlic, minced
- 4 cups low-sodium vegetable broth
- 1/4 cup heavy cream
- 1 tbsp olive oil
- Black pepper

Instructions:

1. In a large pot, heat olive oil over medium heat. Add onions and garlic, cooking until soft.

2. Add cauliflower and vegetable broth. Bring to a boil, then simmer until cauliflower is tender.

3. Puree the soup until smooth. Stir in heavy cream and season with black pepper.

Nutritional Information:

- Calories: 110
- Sodium: 80 mg
- Potassium: 250 mg
- Phosphorus: 55 mg

Quinoa and Black Bean Salad

Ingredients:

- 1 cup cooked quinoa
- 1/2 cup canned black beans, rinsed and drained
- 1 cup diced bell peppers
- 1/4 cup chopped fresh cilantro
- 2 tbsp lime juice
- 1 tbsp olive oil
- Black pepper

Instructions:

1. In a large bowl, combine quinoa, black beans, bell peppers, and cilantro.
2. In a small bowl, whisk together lime juice, olive oil, and black pepper.

Pour over the salad and toss to combine.

Nutritional Information:

- Calories: 120
- Sodium: 15 mg
- Potassium: 220 mg
- Phosphorus: 100 mg

Spinach and Strawberry Salad

Ingredients:

- 3 cups fresh spinach leaves
- 1 cup sliced strawberries
- 1/4 cup sliced almonds
- 2 tbsp balsamic glaze
- Black pepper

Instructions:

1. In a large bowl, combine spinach, strawberries, and almonds.

2. Drizzle with balsamic glaze and toss lightly. Season with black pepper.

Nutritional Information:

- Calories: 80
- Sodium: 20 mg
- Potassium: 220 mg
- Phosphorus: 60 mg

Pumpkin Soup

Ingredients:

- 2 cups pumpkin puree (not pie filling)
- 1/2 cup diced onions
- 4 cups low-sodium vegetable broth

- 1 tsp ground cinnamon
- 1/2 tsp ground nutmeg
- 1/4 cup heavy cream
- 1 tbsp olive oil
- Black pepper

Instructions:

1. In a large pot, heat olive oil over medium heat. Add onions, cooking until translucent.
2. Add pumpkin puree, vegetable broth, cinnamon, and nutmeg. Bring to a boil, then simmer for 20 minutes.
3. Puree the soup until smooth. Stir in heavy cream and season with black pepper.

Nutritional Information:

- Calories: 100

- Sodium: 80 mg
- Potassium: 240 mg
- Phosphorus: 50 mg

Pear and Walnut Salad

Ingredients:

- 3 cups mixed greens (e.g., lettuce, spinach)
- 1 ripe pear, thinly sliced
- 1/4 cup walnuts, chopped
- 1/4 cup crumbled feta cheese
- 2 tbsp olive oil
- 1 tbsp apple cider vinegar
- Black pepper to taste

Instructions:

1. In a large bowl, combine mixed greens, pear slices, walnuts, and feta cheese.

2. In a small bowl, whisk together olive oil and apple cider vinegar. Drizzle over the salad.

3. Toss gently to combine. Season with black pepper to taste.

Nutritional Information:

- Calories: 160
- Sodium: 85 mg
- Potassium: 175 mg
- Phosphorus: 60 mg

Asparagus Lemon Soup

Ingredients:

- 1 lb asparagus, trimmed and cut into pieces
- 4 cups low-sodium chicken or vegetable broth
- 1/2 cup chopped onions
- 1 clove garlic, minced
- 2 tbsp lemon juice
- 1 tsp olive oil
- Black pepper to taste

Instructions:

1. In a large pot, heat olive oil over medium heat. Add onions and garlic, and sauté until soft.

2. Add asparagus and broth. Bring to a boil, then simmer until asparagus is tender, about 15 minutes.

3. Puree the soup with an immersion blender until smooth. Stir in lemon juice.

4. Season with black pepper to taste.

Nutritional Information:

- Calories: 80
- Sodium: 70 mg
- Potassium: 230 mg
- Phosphorus: 55 mg

Mediterranean Chickpea Salad

Ingredients:

- 1 cup canned chickpeas, rinsed and drained

- 1 cup diced cucumbers
- 1 cup diced tomatoes
- 1/4 cup diced red onions
- 1/4 cup chopped parsley
- 2 tbsp olive oil
- 1 tbsp lemon juice
- Black pepper to taste

Instructions:

1. In a large bowl, combine chickpeas, cucumbers, tomatoes, red onions, and parsley.
2. In a small bowl, whisk together olive oil and lemon juice. Drizzle over the salad.
3. Toss to combine. Season with black pepper to taste.

Nutritional Information:

- Calories: 150
- Sodium: 100 mg
- Potassium: 200 mg
- Phosphorus: 120 mg

Broccoli and Cauliflower Soup

Ingredients:

- 2 cups chopped broccoli
- 2 cups chopped cauliflower
- 4 cups low-sodium vegetable broth
- 1/2 cup chopped onions
- 1 clove garlic, minced
- 1/4 cup milk (choose non-dairy for lower phosphorus)
- 1 tsp olive oil

- Black pepper to taste

Instructions:

1. In a large pot, heat olive oil over medium heat. Add onions and garlic, and sauté until translucent.

2. Add broccoli, cauliflower, and broth. Bring to a boil, then simmer until vegetables are tender.

3. Puree the soup until smooth. Stir in milk.

4. Season with black pepper to taste.

Nutritional Information:

- Calories: 90
- Sodium: 60 mg
- Potassium: 300 mg
- Phosphorus: 50 mg

Avocado and Shrimp Salad

Ingredients:

- 2 cups mixed greens
- 1/2 ripe avocado, sliced
- 4 oz cooked shrimp, peeled
- 1/4 cup sliced red bell pepper
- 2 tbsp lime juice
- 1 tbsp olive oil
- Black pepper to taste

Instructions:

1. Arrange mixed greens on a plate. Top with avocado slices, shrimp, and red bell pepper.
2. In a small bowl, whisk together lime juice and olive oil. Drizzle over the salad.

3. Season with black pepper to taste.

Nutritional Information:

- Calories: 220
- Sodium: 85 mg
- Potassium: 350 mg
- Phosphorus: 120 mg

Chapter 8

Main Courses

Beef and Broccoli Stir-Fry

Ingredients:

- 1 pound lean beef, thinly sliced
- 2 cups broccoli florets
- 1 tablespoon olive oil
- 2 cloves garlic, minced
- 1 tablespoon low-sodium soy sauce
- 1 tablespoon oyster sauce
- 1 teaspoon cornstarch
- 1/2 cup water

Instructions:

1. In a pan, heat olive oil over medium heat and sauté garlic until fragrant.
2. Add beef and cook until browned.
3. Mix cornstarch and water, then add to the pan with soy sauce and oyster sauce.

4. Add broccoli and cook until tender.

Nutritional Information:
- Calories: 240
- Sodium: 150 mg
- Potassium: 350 mg
- Phosphorus: 220 mg

Quinoa Vegetable Salad

Ingredients:
- 1 cup quinoa
- 2 cups water
- 1 cup diced cucumbers
- 1 cup cherry tomatoes, halved
- 1/2 cup diced red bell pepper
- 1/4 cup chopped fresh parsley
- 2 tablespoons olive oil
- 1 tablespoon lemon juice
- Salt (optional) and pepper to taste

Instructions:
1. Rinse quinoa under cold water.

2. In a saucepan, bring quinoa and water to a boil. Reduce heat, cover, and simmer for 15 minutes.
3. Let quinoa cool, then mix with vegetables, parsley, olive oil, and lemon juice.

Nutritional Information:
- Calories: 210
- Sodium: 30 mg
- Potassium: 320 mg
- Phosphorus: 150 mg

Grilled Salmon with Dill

Ingredients:
- 4 salmon fillets
- 2 tablespoons olive oil
- 1 tablespoon fresh dill, chopped
- 1 teaspoon lemon zest
- Salt (optional) and pepper to taste

Instructions:

1. Preheat the grill to medium-high heat.
2. Mix olive oil, dill, lemon zest, and pepper. Brush on salmon.
3. Grill salmon, skin-side down, for 6-8 minutes or until done.

Nutritional Information:

- Calories: 280
- Sodium: 80 mg
- Potassium: 500 mg
- Phosphorus: 250 mg

Turkey Vegetable Soup

Ingredients:

- 1 pound ground turkey
- 1 cup diced carrots
- 1 cup diced celery
- 1 cup diced onion
- 2 cloves garlic, minced

- 1 teaspoon olive oil
- 4 cups low-sodium chicken broth
- 1 teaspoon dried thyme
- 1 teaspoon dried rosemary
- Salt (optional) and pepper to taste

Instructions:

1. In a large pot, heat olive oil and sauté onion, garlic, carrots, and celery until soft.
2. Add ground turkey and cook until browned.
3. Add chicken broth, thyme, rosemary, and pepper. Simmer for 30 minutes.

Nutritional Information:

- Calories: 180
- Sodium: 120 mg
- Potassium: 300 mg
- Phosphorus: 200 mg

Pasta Primavera

Ingredients:

- 2 cups cooked whole wheat pasta
- 1 cup steamed broccoli florets
- 1/2 cup sliced carrots
- 1/2 cup diced red bell pepper
- 1/4 cup low-sodium vegetable broth
- 1 tablespoon olive oil
- 2 cloves garlic, minced
- 1 teaspoon dried basil
- Salt (optional) and pepper to taste

Instructions:

1. In a large skillet, heat olive oil and sauté garlic until fragrant.
2. Add vegetables and cook until tender.
3. Add cooked pasta, vegetable broth, basil, and pepper. Stir until heated through.

Nutritional Information:

- Calories: 220
- Sodium: 85 mg
- Potassium: 280 mg
- Phosphorus: 150 mg

Baked Tilapia with Lemon Pepper

Ingredients:

- 4 tilapia fillets
- 2 tablespoons olive oil
- 1 teaspoon lemon pepper seasoning
- 1 tablespoon lemon juice

Instructions:

1. Preheat oven to 400°F (200°C).
2. Place tilapia on a baking sheet. Brush with olive oil, and lemon juice, and sprinkle with lemon pepper.
3. Bake for 12-15 minutes or until fish flakes easily.

Nutritional Information:

- Calories: 145
- Sodium: 55 mg
- Potassium: 330 mg
- Phosphorus: 170 mg

Cauliflower Rice Stir-Fry

Ingredients:

- 1 head cauliflower, grated into "rice"
- 1 cup mixed vegetables (peas, carrots, corn)
- 1 tablespoon olive oil
- 2 cloves garlic, minced
- 1 tablespoon low-sodium soy sauce
- 1 egg, beaten (optional)
- Salt (optional) and pepper to taste

Instructions:

1. Heat olive oil in a large skillet over medium heat. Sauté garlic until fragrant.

2. Add cauliflower rice and vegetables. Cook for 5-7 minutes.
3. Push rice to the side, add beaten egg to the other side, and scramble. Mix everything.
4. Stir in soy sauce and serve.

Nutritional Information:
- Calories: 120
- Sodium: 90 mg
- Potassium: 320 mg
- Phosphorus: 150 mg

Grilled Veggie Platter

Ingredients:
- 1 zucchini, sliced
- 1 yellow squash, sliced
- 1 red bell pepper, sliced
- 1 tablespoon olive oil
- Salt (optional) and pepper to taste

Instructions:
1. Preheat the grill to medium-high heat.
2. Toss vegetables with olive oil and pepper.
3. Grill vegetables until tender and slightly charred, about 5 minutes per side.

Nutritional Information:
- Calories: 80
- Sodium: 25 mg
- Potassium: 290 mg
- Phosphorus: 60 mg

Chicken and Rice Casserole

Ingredients:
- 1 cup cooked white rice
- 2 cups cooked, shredded chicken breast

- 1 cup low-sodium cream of mushroom soup
- 1/2 cup peas
- 1/2 cup carrots, diced
- 1/2 cup water
- Salt (optional) and pepper to taste

Instructions:
1. Preheat oven to 350°F (175°C).
2. In a casserole dish, mix all ingredients thoroughly.
3. Bake for 30 minutes or until bubbly.

Nutritional Information:
- Calories: 210
- Sodium: 95 mg
- Potassium: 220 mg
- Phosphorus: 180 mg

Tuna Salad with Greek Yogurt

Ingredients:
- 1 can (5 oz) low-sodium tuna, drained

- 1/4 cup Greek yogurt
- 1/4 cup diced celery
- 1/4 cup diced apple
- 1 tablespoon lemon juice
- Salt (optional) and pepper to taste

Instructions:

1. In a bowl, mix all ingredients until well combined.
2. Serve chilled with whole-grain crackers or on a bed of lettuce.

Nutritional Information:

- Calories: 130
- Sodium: 70 mg
- Potassium: 150 mg
- Phosphorus: 120 mg

Baked Cod with Tomatoes and Olives

Ingredients:

- 4 cod fillets
- 1 cup cherry tomatoes, halved

- 1/4 cup olives, pitted and sliced
- 2 tablespoons olive oil
- 1 teaspoon dried oregano
- Salt (optional) and pepper to taste

Instructions:

1. Preheat oven to 375°F (190°C).
2. Place cod in a baking dish. Top with tomatoes, olives, olive oil, oregano, and pepper.
3. Bake for 20-25 minutes or until the cod is flaky.

Nutritional Information:

- Calories: 200
- Sodium: 85 mg
- Potassium: 450 mg
- Phosphorus: 190 mg

Vegetable Quiche (Crustless)

Ingredients:

- 1 cup low-fat milk

- 4 eggs
- 1 cup chopped spinach
- 1/2 cup diced mushrooms
- 1/2 cup shredded low-sodium cheese
- Salt (optional) and pepper to taste

Instructions:
1. Preheat oven to 350°F (175°C).
2. Whisk together milk and eggs. Stir in spinach, mushrooms, and cheese.
3. Pour into a greased pie dish and bake for 45 minutes or until set.

Nutritional Information:
- Calories: 140
- Sodium: 120 mg
- Potassium: 200 mg
- Phosphorus: 150 mg

Lentil Soup

Ingredients:

- 1 cup lentils, rinsed
- 4 cups low-sodium vegetable broth
- 1 cup diced tomatoes
- 1 cup diced carrots
- 1 cup diced celery
- 1 teaspoon olive oil
- 1 teaspoon cumin
- Salt (optional) and pepper to taste

Instructions:

1. In a large pot, heat olive oil over medium heat. Add carrots and celery; cook until soft.
2. Add lentils, broth, tomatoes, cumin, and pepper. Bring to a boil, then simmer for 30 minutes or until lentils are tender.

Nutritional Information:

- Calories: 180

- Sodium: 90 mg
- Potassium: 370 mg
- Phosphorus: 180 mg

Shrimp and Zucchini Noodles

Ingredients:
- 1 pound shrimp, peeled and deveined
- 2 medium zucchinis, spiralized
- 1 tablespoon olive oil
- 2 cloves garlic, minced
- 1 teaspoon chili flakes (optional)
- 1 tablespoon lemon juice
- Salt (optional) and pepper to taste

Instructions:
1. In a pan, heat olive oil over medium heat. Add garlic and chili flakes; sauté until fragrant.
2. Add shrimp and cook until pink.

3. Toss in zucchini noodles and lemon juice; cook until zucchini is tender.

Nutritional Information:
- Calories: 180
- Sodium: 120 mg
- Potassium: 320 mg
- Phosphorus: 220 mg

Chapter 9

Sides and Sauces

Cauliflower Mash

Ingredients:

- 1 head cauliflower, cut into florets
- 2 tbsp unsalted butter
- 2 tbsp light cream (optional)
- Salt (minimal) and pepper to taste

Instructions:

1. Steam the cauliflower florets until very tender, about 10 minutes.
2. Transfer the cauliflower to a blender or food processor. Add butter, cream (if using), and a pinch of salt and pepper.

3. Blend until smooth and creamy. Adjust seasoning if necessary.

Nutritional Information:

- Low in potassium and phosphorus.
- Sodium: minimal, adjusted according to dietary needs.

Carrot and Zucchini Ribbons

Ingredients:

- 2 medium carrots
- 2 medium zucchinis
- 1 tbsp olive oil
- Salt (minimal) and pepper to taste
- Fresh herbs (e.g., parsley or dill) for garnish

Instructions:

1. Use a vegetable peeler to slice the carrots and zucchini into thin ribbons.

2. Heat olive oil in a pan over medium heat. Add the vegetable ribbons, tossing gently. Season with a minimal amount of salt and pepper.

3. Cook until vegetables are slightly tender, about 3-5 minutes. Garnish with fresh herbs before serving.

Nutritional Information:

- Low in potassium, phosphorus, and sodium.

Green Bean Almondine

Ingredients:

- 1 lb green beans, trimmed
- 1 tbsp olive oil

- 2 tbsp slivered almonds
- 1 tsp lemon juice
- Salt (minimal) and pepper to taste

Instructions:

1. Blanch the green beans in boiling water for 3 minutes, then plunge into ice water to stop the cooking process.
2. In a skillet, heat olive oil over medium heat. Add almonds and toast lightly.
3. Add green beans and sauté until heated through. Season with lemon juice, a pinch of salt, and pepper.
4. Serve warm.

Nutritional Information:

- Low in potassium and phosphorus.

Lemon-Dill Sauce

Ingredients:

- 1/2 cup low-fat Greek yogurt
- 1 tbsp fresh dill, chopped
- 1 tsp lemon zest
- 1 tbsp lemon juice
- Salt (minimal) and pepper to taste

Instructions:

1. In a bowl, combine Greek yogurt, dill, lemon zest, and lemon juice. Mix well.
2. Season with a pinch of salt and pepper to taste.
3. Serve with grilled or baked fish, chicken, or vegetables.

Nutritional Information:

- Low in potassium, phosphorus, and sodium. High in protein.

Apple Cucumber Salad

Ingredients:

- 1 large cucumber, thinly sliced
- 1 apple, thinly sliced
- 1 tbsp apple cider vinegar
- 1 tsp olive oil
- Fresh mint leaves, chopped
- Salt (minimal) and pepper to taste

Instructions:

1. In a large bowl, combine the cucumber and apple slices.

2. In a small bowl, whisk together apple cider vinegar, olive oil, chopped mint, and a pinch of salt and pepper.

3. Pour the dressing over the cucumber and apple slices. Toss gently to coat.

4. Refrigerate for at least 30 minutes before serving.

Nutritional Information:

- Low in potassium, phosphorus, and sodium.

Garlic Olive Oil Pasta

Ingredients:

- 2 cups cooked pasta (preferably a low-sodium variety)
- 2 tbsp olive oil
- 2 garlic cloves, minced
- Fresh parsley, chopped

- Salt (minimal) and pepper to taste

Instructions:

1. Heat olive oil in a pan over medium heat. Add minced garlic and sauté until fragrant.

2. Add the cooked pasta to the pan and toss to coat with the garlic olive oil.

3. Season with a pinch of salt and pepper. Garnish with fresh parsley before serving.

Nutritional Information:

- Low in potassium and phosphorus. Sodium content depends on the pasta brand; choose low-sodium options.

Honey Mustard Dressing

Ingredients:

- 1/4 cup Dijon mustard (low sodium)
- 2 tbsp honey
- 1 tbsp apple cider vinegar
- 1 tbsp olive oil
- Salt (minimal) and pepper to taste

Instructions:

1. In a bowl, whisk together Dijon mustard, honey, apple cider vinegar, and olive oil.
2. Season with a minimal amount of salt and pepper. Adjust according to taste.
3. Serve with salads or as a dipping sauce for vegetables.

Nutritional Information:

- Low in potassium and phosphorus. Be mindful of sodium in mustard and adjust the amount used as necessary.

Roasted Bell Peppers

Ingredients:

- 4 bell peppers (mixed colors), sliced
- 1 tbsp olive oil
- Salt (minimal) and pepper to taste

Instructions:

1. Preheat oven to 425°F (220°C).
2. Toss bell pepper slices with olive oil, a pinch of salt, and pepper.
3. Spread on a baking sheet in a single layer. Roast for 20-25 minutes, until tender and slightly charred.

4. Serve as a side dish or add to salads.

Nutritional Information:

- Low in potassium, phosphorus, and sodium.

Balsamic Vinaigrette

Ingredients:

- 3 tbsp balsamic vinegar
- 1 tbsp olive oil
- 1 tsp honey
- Salt (minimal) and pepper to taste

Instructions:

1. In a small bowl, whisk together balsamic vinegar, olive oil, and honey.
2. Season with a pinch of salt and pepper. Adjust to taste.

3. Use as a dressing for salads or a marinade for vegetables.

Nutritional Information:

- Low in potassium and phosphorus. Monitor sodium intake elsewhere in your diet.

Mashed Sweet Potatoes

Ingredients:

- 2 medium sweet potatoes, peeled and cubed
- 1 tbsp unsalted butter
- 1/4 cup milk (low-fat or non-dairy alternative)
- Salt (minimal) and pepper to taste
- A pinch of cinnamon (optional)

Instructions:

1. Boil sweet potatoes in water until tender, about 15 minutes. Drain well.

2. Mash the sweet potatoes with butter and milk until smooth. Season with a pinch of salt, pepper, and cinnamon if using.

3. Serve warm as a side dish.

Nutritional Information:

- Moderate in potassium. Low in phosphorus and sodium.

Cilantro Lime Rice

Ingredients:

- 1 cup long-grain white rice
- 2 cups water
- 1/4 cup fresh lime juice

- 1/2 cup chopped cilantro
- 1 tbsp olive oil
- Salt (minimal) and pepper to taste

Instructions:

1. Bring water to a boil in a saucepan. Add rice and stir. Reduce heat to low, cover, and simmer until water is absorbed, about 18 minutes.
2. Remove from heat. Let it stand covered for 5 minutes.
3. Fluff rice with a fork. Stir in lime juice, cilantro, and olive oil. Season with a pinch of salt and pepper.
4. Serve as a flavorful side dish.

Nutritional Information:

- Low in potassium and phosphorus. Control sodium by limiting salt.

Tangy Coleslaw

Ingredients:

- 4 cups shredded cabbage (red or green)
- 1 carrot, shredded
- 1/4 cup apple cider vinegar
- 2 tbsp olive oil
- 1 tbsp honey or sugar substitute
- Salt (minimal) and pepper to taste

Instructions:

1. In a large bowl, combine shredded cabbage and carrot.
2. In a small bowl, whisk together apple cider vinegar, olive oil, and honey or sugar substitute.

3. Pour the dressing over the cabbage mixture and toss to coat evenly. Season with a pinch of salt and pepper.

4. Chill in the refrigerator for at least 1 hour before serving to allow flavors to meld.

Nutritional Information:

- Low in potassium, phosphorus, and sodium. A good source of fiber.

Basil Pesto (Low Sodium)

Ingredients:

- 2 cups fresh basil leaves
- 1/4 cup pine nuts or walnuts
- 2 garlic cloves
- 1/4 cup grated Parmesan cheese (low sodium)

- 1/2 cup olive oil
- Pepper to taste

Instructions:

1. In a food processor, combine basil leaves, nuts, garlic, and Parmesan cheese. Pulse until coarsely chopped.
2. With the processor running, gradually add olive oil until the mixture is smooth.
3. Season with pepper to taste. Use minimal or no salt.
4. Serve with pasta or as a spread on sandwiches.

Nutritional Information:

- Low in potassium and phosphorus. Be mindful of the cheese's sodium content; choose a low-sodium variety.

Quinoa Salad with Lemon Vinaigrette

Ingredients:

- 1 cup quinoa, rinsed
- 2 cups water
- 1 cucumber, diced
- 1 bell pepper, diced
- 1/4 cup red onion, finely chopped
- 1/4 cup fresh lemon juice
- 1/4 cup olive oil
- Salt (minimal) and pepper to taste
- Fresh herbs (e.g., parsley) for garnish

Instructions:

1. In a saucepan, bring water to a boil. Add quinoa, reduce heat to low, cover, and simmer until quinoa is tender and water is absorbed about 15 minutes. Let cool.

2. In a large bowl, combine cooled quinoa, cucumber, bell pepper, and red onion.

3. In a small bowl, whisk together lemon juice and olive oil. Season with a pinch of salt and pepper.

4. Pour dressing over the quinoa mixture and toss to combine. Garnish with fresh herbs.

5. Serve chilled or at room temperature.

Nutritional Information:

- Low in sodium, potassium, and phosphorus. Quinoa provides high-quality protein.

Steamed Asparagus with Lemon Butter

Ingredients:

- 1 lb asparagus, trimmed
- 2 tbsp unsalted butter, melted
- 1 tbsp lemon juice
- Lemon zest for garnish
- Salt (minimal) and pepper to taste

Instructions:

1. Steam asparagus until tender-crisp, about 3-5 minutes.
2. In a small bowl, mix melted butter and lemon juice.

3. Drizzle the lemon butter over the steamed asparagus. Season with a pinch of salt and pepper.

4. Garnish with lemon zest before serving.

Nutritional Information:

- Low in potassium, phosphorus, and sodium.

Chapter 10

Desserts and Treats

Low-Potassium Apple Crisp

Ingredients:

- 4 medium apples, peeled and sliced
- 1/2 cup brown sugar
- 1/2 cup all-purpose flour
- 1/2 cup quick-cooking oats
- 1/3 cup unsalted butter, melted
- 1/2 teaspoon ground cinnamon
- 1/4 teaspoon ground nutmeg

Instructions:

1. Preheat oven to 350°F (175°C).
2. Place apples in an 8-inch square baking dish.
3. In a bowl, combine brown sugar, flour, oats, butter, cinnamon, and nutmeg. Sprinkle over apples.

4. Bake for 30 minutes, until the topping is golden and the apples are tender.

Nutritional Information:
- Calories: 210
- Sodium: 20 mg
- Potassium: 150 mg
- Phosphorus: 50 mg

Vanilla Rice Pudding

Ingredients:
- 1 cup cooked white rice
- 2 cups low-fat milk
- 1/4 cup sugar
- 1/2 teaspoon vanilla extract
- Cinnamon for garnish (optional)

Instructions:
1. In a saucepan, combine all ingredients except cinnamon. Cook over medium heat, stirring until thickened, about 15-20 minutes.

2. Chill in the refrigerator. Serve with a sprinkle of cinnamon if desired.

Nutritional Information:
- Calories: 180
- Sodium: 60 mg
- Potassium: 90 mg
- Phosphorus: 100 mg

Lemon Bars

Ingredients:
- 1 cup all-purpose flour
- 1/4 cup powdered sugar
- 1/2 cup unsalted butter
- 2 large eggs
- 1 cup granulated sugar
- 2 tablespoons all-purpose flour
- 3 tablespoons lemon juice

Instructions:
1. Preheat oven to 350°F (175°C).

2. Blend 1 cup flour, powdered sugar, and butter until crumbly. Press into the bottom of an ungreased 8x8-inch pan.
3. Bake for 20 minutes. Then, whisk together eggs, granulated sugar, 2 tablespoons flour, and lemon juice. Pour over baked crust.
4. Bake for an additional 25 minutes. Cool and dust with powdered sugar.

Nutritional Information:
- Calories: 160
- Sodium: 20 mg
- Potassium: 30 mg
- Phosphorus: 40 mg

Kidney-Friendly Chocolate Cake

Ingredients:
- 1 cup all-purpose flour
- 1 cup granulated sugar

- 1/4 cup unsweetened cocoa powder
- 1/4 cup unsalted butter
- 1/2 cup low-fat milk
- 1 teaspoon vanilla extract
- 1/2 teaspoon baking soda

Instructions:
1. Preheat oven to 350°F (175°C). Grease a 9-inch round cake pan.
2. In a bowl, mix flour, sugar, cocoa, and baking soda. Add butter, milk, and vanilla; mix until smooth.
3. Pour into the prepared pan. Bake for 30 minutes. Cool before serving.

Nutritional Information:
- Calories: 220
- Sodium: 75 mg
- Potassium: 110 mg
- Phosphorus: 60 mg

Berry Fruit Salad

Ingredients:

- 1 cup strawberries, sliced
- 1 cup blueberries
- 1 cup raspberries
- 2 tablespoons honey
- 1 teaspoon fresh lemon juice

Instructions:

1. Combine all berries in a large bowl.
2. Drizzle with honey and lemon juice; gently toss to coat.

Nutritional Information:

- Calories: 90
- Sodium: 5 mg
- Potassium: 120 mg
- Phosphorus: 35 mg

Peach Sorbet

Ingredients:

- 4 ripe peaches, peeled and diced

- 1/2 cup sugar (or sugar substitute)
- 1 tablespoon lemon juice

Instructions:

1. Puree peaches, sugar, and lemon juice in a blender until smooth.
2. Freeze in an ice cream maker according to the manufacturer's instructions, or pour into a container and freeze, stirring every 30 minutes until set.

Nutritional Information:

- Calories: 120
- Sodium: 0 mg
- Potassium: 190 mg
- Phosphorus: 10 mg

Almond Biscotti

Ingredients:

- 2 cups all-purpose flour
- 3/4 cup sugar

- 1 teaspoon baking powder
- 1/4 cup unsalted butter, melted
- 2 eggs
- 1 teaspoon almond extract
- 1/2 cup sliced almonds

Instructions:
1. Preheat oven to 350°F (175°C). Line a baking sheet with parchment paper.
2. Mix flour, sugar, and baking powder. Stir in butter, eggs, and almond extract until dough forms. Fold in almonds.
3. Form the dough into a log on the prepared baking sheet. Bake for 25 minutes, then cool slightly and slice. Bake slices again until toasted.

Nutritional Information:
- Calories: 160
- Sodium: 20 mg
- Potassium: 45 mg

- Phosphorus: 60 mg

Carrot Cake Muffins

Ingredients:

- 1 1/2 cups all-purpose flour
- 1/2 cup sugar
- 1 teaspoon baking soda
- 1 teaspoon ground cinnamon
- 1/4 cup unsweetened applesauce
- 2 tablespoons canola oil
- 2 large eggs
- 1 1/2 cups grated carrots

Instructions:

1. Preheat oven to 350°F (175°C). Line a muffin tin with paper liners.
2. In a large bowl, mix flour, sugar, baking soda, and cinnamon. In another bowl, whisk applesauce, oil, and eggs. Stir into dry ingredients until just moistened. Fold in carrots.

3. Fill muffin cups three-fourths full. Bake for 20-25 minutes.

Nutritional Information:
- Calories: 130
- Sodium: 115 mg
- Potassium: 90 mg
- Phosphorus: 40 mg

Coconut Macaroons

Ingredients:
- 2 1/2 cups shredded unsweetened coconut
- 3/4 cup sugar
- 2 egg whites
- 1 teaspoon vanilla extract

Instructions:
1. Preheat oven to 325°F (165°C). Line a baking sheet with parchment paper.

2. Mix all ingredients in a bowl until well combined. Drop by spoonfuls onto the prepared baking sheet.
3. Bake for 20-25 minutes until golden. Let cool on a wire rack.

Nutritional Information:
- Calories: 100
- Sodium: 25 mg
- Potassium: 80 mg
- Phosphorus: 20 mg

Angel Food Cake

Ingredients:
- 1 cup cake flour
- 1 1/2 cups sugar
- 12 egg whites
- 1 teaspoon cream of tartar
- 1 teaspoon vanilla extract

Instructions:
1. Preheat oven to 350°F (175°C).

2. Sift flour and 3/4 cup sugar together three times. In a large bowl, beat egg whites with cream of tartar until soft peaks form. Gradually add the remaining sugar, then vanilla, beating until stiff peaks form. Fold in flour mixture.
3. Pour into an ungreased 10-inch tube pan. Bake for 40 minutes. Invert the pan to cool completely.

Nutritional Information:
- Calories: 140
- Sodium: 85 mg
- Potassium: 45 mg
- Phosphorus: 10 mg

Pumpkin Spice Muffins

Ingredients:
- 1 1/2 cups all-purpose flour
- 1/2 cup sugar

- 2 teaspoons baking powder
- 1/2 teaspoon cinnamon
- 1/4 teaspoon nutmeg
- 1/4 teaspoon ginger
- 1/2 cup unsweetened applesauce
- 1/2 cup canned pumpkin (not pumpkin pie filling)
- 1/4 cup low-fat milk
- 1 egg

Instructions:

1. Preheat oven to 350°F (175°C). Line a muffin tin with paper liners.
2. In a large bowl, combine flour, sugar, baking powder, cinnamon, nutmeg, and ginger. In another bowl, mix applesauce, pumpkin, milk, and egg. Stir wet ingredients into dry until just moistened.
3. Fill muffin cups three-fourths full. Bake for 22-25 minutes.

Nutritional Information:
- Calories: 110
- Sodium: 75 mg
- Potassium: 90 mg
- Phosphorus: 60 mg

Pear and Ginger Crumble

Ingredients:
- 4 ripe pears, peeled and sliced
- 2 tablespoons brown sugar
- 1 teaspoon ground ginger
- 3/4 cup quick-cooking oats
- 1/4 cup flour
- 1/4 cup unsalted butter, melted
- 1/4 cup chopped walnuts (optional)

Instructions:
1. Preheat oven to 350°F (175°C).
2. Toss pears with brown sugar and ginger; place in a baking dish.

3. Mix oats, flour, and butter until crumbly; stir in walnuts if using. Sprinkle over pears.
4. Bake for 30 minutes, until the topping is golden and the pears are tender.

Nutritional Information:
- Calories: 180
- Sodium: 5 mg
- Potassium: 150 mg
- Phosphorus: 40 mg

Strawberry Gelatin Parfait

Ingredients:
- 1 package of sugar-free strawberry gelatin
- 2 cups boiling water
- 1 cup sliced strawberries
- 1 cup low-fat vanilla yogurt

Instructions:
1. Dissolve gelatin in boiling water. Chill until slightly thickened.
2. Layer gelatin, strawberries, and yogurt in glasses. Chill until set.

Nutritional Information:
- Calories: 90
- Sodium: 55 mg
- Potassium: 110 mg
- Phosphorus: 45 mg

Chocolate Peanut Butter Balls

Ingredients:
- 1 cup powdered milk
- 1/2 cup unsweetened cocoa powder
- 1/2 cup natural peanut butter
- 1/2 cup honey

Instructions:

1. In a bowl, mix powdered milk and cocoa powder. Stir in peanut butter and honey until well combined.
2. Roll mixture into balls. Place on a baking sheet lined with parchment paper and refrigerate until firm.

Nutritional Information:

- Calories: 100
- Sodium: 60 mg
- Potassium: 150 mg
- Phosphorus: 100 mg

Blueberry Lemon Muffins

Ingredients:

- 2 cups all-purpose flour
- 1/2 cup sugar
- 3 teaspoons baking powder
- 1/2 teaspoon salt
- 3/4 cup low-fat milk

- 1/4 cup vegetable oil
- 1 egg
- 1 teaspoon grated lemon zest
- 1 cup fresh blueberries

Instructions:

1. Preheat oven to 400°F (200°C). Line a muffin tin with paper liners.
2. In a large bowl, combine flour, sugar, baking powder, and salt. In another bowl, mix milk, oil, egg, and lemon zest. Stir into dry ingredients just until moistened. Fold in blueberries.
3. Fill muffin cups two-thirds full. Bake for 20-25 minutes.

Nutritional Information:

- Calories: 150
- Sodium: 100 mg
- Potassium: 85 mg
- Phosphorus: 80 mg

Chapter 11

Beverages and Smoothies

Cranberry Apple Spritzer

Ingredients:

- 1 cup cranberry juice (low sugar)
- 1 cup sparkling water
- 1/2 cup apple juice (low sugar)
- Ice cubes

Instructions:

1. In a large glass, combine cranberry juice and apple juice.
2. Fill the glass with ice cubes, then top off with sparkling water.
3. Stir gently and serve immediately.

Nutritional Information:

Low in potassium and phosphorus.

Blueberry Lemonade Smoothie

Ingredients:

- 1/2 cup blueberries (fresh or frozen)
- 1 cup lemonade (low sugar)
- 1/2 cup ice
- 1 tbsp honey (optional)

Instructions:

1. In a blender, combine blueberries, lemonade, ice, and honey if using.
2. Blend until smooth.
3. Serve immediately in a chilled glass.

Nutritional Information:

Low in potassium and phosphorus.

Cucumber Mint Water

Ingredients:

- 1 liter water
- 1 cucumber, thinly sliced
- 10 mint leaves

Instructions:

1. In a large pitcher, combine water, cucumber slices, and mint leaves.
2. Refrigerate for at least 1 hour to allow flavors to infuse.
3. Serve chilled with ice if desired.

Nutritional Information:

- Very low in potassium, phosphorus, and sodium.

Peach Iced Tea (Low Sugar)

Ingredients:

- 4 decaffeinated tea bags
- 4 cups boiling water
- 1 peach, sliced
- Sweetener of choice (optional, to taste)

Instructions:

1. Steep tea bags in boiling water for 5 minutes. Remove the tea bags and let the tea cool.
2. In a pitcher, combine cooled tea and peach slices.

3. Refrigerate until chilled. Sweeten to taste if desired.

4. Serve over ice.

Nutritional Information:

- Low in potassium and phosphorus.

Pineapple Coconut Water

Ingredients:

- 1 cup coconut water (low sodium)
- 1/2 cup pineapple juice (low sugar)
- Ice cubes

Instructions:

1. In a glass, combine coconut water and pineapple juice.

2. Add ice cubes and stir well.

3. Serve immediately for a tropical refreshment.

Nutritional Information:

- Moderate in potassium, Low in phosphorus and sodium.

Carrot Ginger Juice

Ingredients:

- 2 carrots, peeled and chopped
- 1/2 inch ginger root, peeled
- 1 cup water
- Sweetener of choice (optional, to taste)

Instructions:

1. In a blender, combine carrots, ginger, and water. Blend until smooth.
2. Strain through a fine mesh sieve or cheesecloth.

3. Sweeten to taste if desired. Serve chilled.

Nutritional Information:

- Low in potassium and phosphorus.

Strawberry Basil Water

Ingredients:

- 1 liter water
- 1 cup strawberries, sliced
- 5-6 basil leaves

Instructions:

1. In a large pitcher, combine water, strawberry slices, and basil leaves.
2. Refrigerate for at least 1 hour to infuse.
3. Serve chilled with ice if desired.

Nutritional Information:

- Very low in potassium, phosphorus, and sodium.

Almond Milk Smoothie

Ingredients:

- 1 cup almond milk (unsweetened)
- 1/2 banana (for lower potassium, use half)
- 1/2 cup blueberries (fresh or frozen)
- 1 tbsp almond butter

Instructions:

1. In a blender, combine almond milk, half a banana, blueberries, and almond butter.
2. Blend until smooth.
3. Serve immediately.

Nutritional Information:

- Moderate in potassium, Low in phosphorus and sodium.

Herbal Tea Infusion

Ingredients:

- 1 liter boiling water
- 2 herbal tea bags (e.g., chamomile, peppermint)
- Sweetener of choice (optional, to taste)

Instructions:

1. Steep tea bags in boiling water for 5-10 minutes, depending on desired strength.
2. Remove the tea bags and let the tea cool.

3. Sweeten to taste if desired. Serve chilled or at room temperature.

Nutritional Information:

- Free of potassium, phosphorus, and sodium.

Green Smoothie

Ingredients:

- 1 cup spinach (fresh)
- 1/2 apple, cored and sliced
- 1/2 cup cucumber, sliced
- 1 cup water
- Ice cubes

Instructions:

1. In a blender, combine spinach, apple, cucumber, and water. Blend until smooth.

2. Add ice cubes and blend again until frosty.

3. Serve immediately.

Nutritional Information:

- Low in potassium and phosphorus. High in vitamins and minerals.

Lemon Ginger Zinger

Ingredients:

- 1 liter water
- 1 lemon, juiced
- 1-inch ginger root, grated
- Sweetener of choice (optional, to taste)

Instructions:

1. In a pitcher, combine water, lemon juice, and grated ginger.

2. Refrigerate for at least 1 hour to allow flavors to meld.

3. Sweeten to taste if desired. Serve chilled with ice.

Nutritional Information:

- Low in potassium and phosphorus.

Berry Blast Smoothie

Ingredients:

- 1/2 cup strawberries (fresh or frozen)
- 1/2 cup raspberries (fresh or frozen)
- 1 cup almond milk (unsweetened)
- Sweetener of choice (optional, to taste)

Instructions:

1. In a blender, combine strawberries, raspberries, and almond milk. Blend until smooth.

2. Sweeten to taste if desired.

3. Serve immediately.

Nutritional Information:

- Moderate in potassium, Low in phosphorus and sodium.

Minty Melon Drink

Ingredients:

- 1 cup melon (cantaloupe or honeydew), cubed
- 1 liter water
- 10 mint leaves

Instructions:

1. Blend melon cubes with a little water until smooth.

2. Combine melon puree with the rest of the water in a pitcher. Add mint leaves.

3. Refrigerate for at least 1 hour. Serve chilled.

Nutritional Information:

- Moderate in potassium, Low in phosphorus and sodium.

Iced Hibiscus Tea

Ingredients:

- 4 hibiscus tea bags
- 4 cups boiling water
- Sweetener of choice (optional, to taste)

- Lemon slices for garnish

Instructions:

1. Steep tea bags in boiling water for 5 minutes.//
2. Remove tea bags and let cool. Sweeten to taste if desired.
3. Refrigerate until chilled. Serve with lemon slices.

Nutritional Information:

- Low in potassium, phosphorus, and sodium.

Vanilla Almond Shake

Ingredients:

- 1 cup almond milk (unsweetened)
- 1 tsp vanilla extract
- Ice cubes

- Sweetener of choice (optional, to taste)

Instructions:

1. In a blender, combine almond milk, vanilla extract, and ice cubes. Blend until smooth.

2. Sweeten to taste if desired.

3. Serve immediately for a refreshing, creamy treat.

Nutritional Information:

- Low in potassium and phosphorus.

Chapter 12

Conclusion

The "Kidney Dialysis Diet Cookbook for Beginners" offers a comprehensive solution for individuals navigating the complexities of a kidney dialysis diet. Through a careful selection of recipes, beverages, and smoothies, this cookbook provides not only delicious meal options but also invaluable nutritional information tailored to the specific needs of those undergoing dialysis.

By focusing on low potassium, low phosphorus, low sodium, and appropriate fluid intake, each recipe in this cookbook ensures that individuals can enjoy flavorful and satisfying meals without compromising their health. From nutrient-rich sides like cauliflower mash to refreshing beverages like cucumber mint water, every dish is crafted to support kidney health while delighting the palate.

Moreover, this cookbook serves as an educational resource, offering insights into the importance of dietary restrictions and practical tips for meal planning. Whether you're a beginner in the kitchen or an experienced cook, the "Kidney Dialysis Diet Cookbook for Beginners" empowers individuals to take control of their diet and embrace a healthier lifestyle.

In conclusion, this cookbook is not just a collection of recipes; it's a guidebook for living well with kidney dialysis. By following the guidance and recipes provided within these pages, individuals can embark on a journey towards improved health and well-being. With the "Kidney Dialysis Diet Cookbook for Beginners" as a trusted companion, navigating the challenges of a kidney dialysis diet becomes not only manageable but also enjoyable, paving the way for a brighter and healthier future.

Manufactured by Amazon.ca
Acheson, AB